My SPACE ATLAS

Words marked with an asterisk* are explained in the glossary at the back of the book.

Written by Alexandre Wajnberg

Editorial direction by Galia Lami Dozo – van der Kar

Illustrated by Vivi & Gus

Translated by Joanna Neville

Page layout by Jérémy Lurquin & Diego Funck

The Universe

Space, and everything about it

Our universe is made up of all sorts of different things: galaxies*, stars and planets that revolve around their own stars like Earth revolves around the Sun. Stars group together in galaxies.

Certain stars explode and die, emitting a flash of light 1000 times brighter than the Sun! We call these stars, supernovae*.

From time to time, comets* pass by. They travel around the Sun, returning every few years. Every now and then, smaller meteorites* also approach Earth.

When they fall through the Earth's atmosphere, they burn. These are known as shooting* stars – whizzzz!

There's nothing you won't find in the Universe. So, are you ready for your great voyage of discovery?

Your place in the Universe

You on Earth

Earth and the other planets of our solar system

The Universe and some of its galaxies

The Universe is expanding!

There are billions of galaxies and they are all moving away from us. The Universe is constantly spreading out. Everything is getting further away and we are not even at the centre of the Universe! It's a bit like a child blowing up a balloon that has dots. As the balloon expands, the dots on the surface move further apart – and none of them are found in the center of the balloon.

1 A planet
2 A comet*
3 A nebula*
4 A galaxy*
5 Another planet
6 A star cluster
7 A supernova*
8 Another galaxy
9 The Sun

The Big Bang

The birth of the Universe

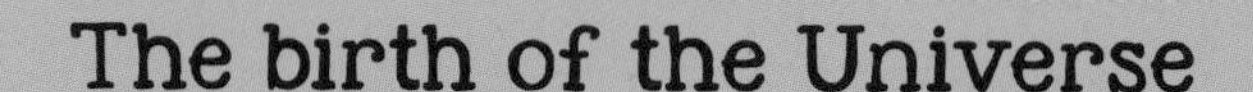

Nobody knows what existed "before". But all of a sudden, out of nowhere, there was a gigantic explosion: the Big Bang. This took place some 14 billion years ago. There was nothing and then, suddenly, in a fraction of a second, matter appeared. And it was hot! Billions of degrees Celsius, in fact. The Universe inflated rapidly as it cooled and huge clouds of gas formed. These clouds were the origins of the galaxies*... billions of galaxies and their stars.

The echo of the Big Bang

The Big Bang's flash of light still resonates today, albeit very weakly, out in space. It takes the form of radio* waves, like an echo of light! Radio waves were discovered in 1964 by Penzias and Wilson, while they were adjusting their radio telescope* to eradicate the noise that they had assumed to be interference! This was serious "proof" that the Big Bang had taken place and won them the Nobel Prize.

1 First there was the Big Bang, which created particles* that would ultimately form matter as we know it.

2 Enormous clouds (mainly hydrogen*) were released as a result of the Big Bang; these were the origins of the galaxies.

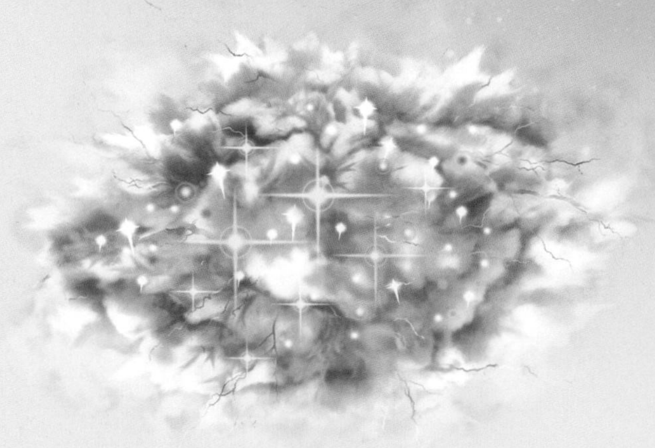

The future of the Universe

The future of the Universe depends on the total amount of matter within it. This is because natural attraction between bodies prevents them from dispersing. If the amount of matter drops too low, the Universe – less firmly held together – will spread out exponentially, slowing down as it does so. Yet we have no idea how much matter there is! On the other hand, if there is too much matter, the Universe's expansion will halt and go into reverse gear – it will contract (increasingly quickly), heat up and end in a terrific implosion (the opposite of an explosion), which has been dubbed the "Big Crunch". Either way, the expansion is due to slow down – yet recent measurements indicate that it is in fact speeding up!?! This throws everything into question!

Galaxies

Clusters of stars

Galaxies are enormous space systems composed of dust, gas and countless stars. In fact, in a single galaxy, you will find billions of them! Galaxies also contain cosmic* dust and gas clouds... and it all stays grouped together, like a massive, slowly rotating flock.

Our galaxy is known as "spiral". It consists of a flat disk with a bulging center and surrounding spiral arms. The galaxy's disk includes stars, planets, dust and gas – all of which rotate around the galactic center in a regular manner. Many galaxies are like this, but not all. There are "elliptical" galaxies (shaped like a rugby ball); "barred spiral" galaxies (with a stretched centre a bit like a thick bar) and finally, "irregular" galaxies. There are more galaxies in the Universe than there are grains of sand in the Sahara desert!

Elliptical galaxy

Spiral galaxy (like ours)

Barred spiral galaxy

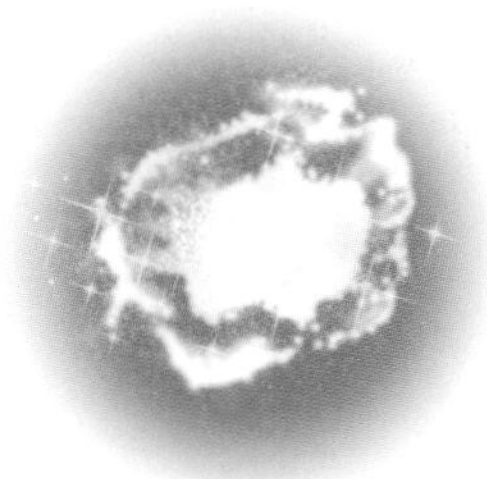

Irregular galaxy

Our neighbouring galaxy: Andromeda

Our galaxy: the Milky Way

If, on a clear summer's night, you gaze up at the night sky, you will notice an area containing more stars than elsewhere. It looks a bit like a path (or line), that divides the sky in two. The ancient Greeks named this the "milky" way since the stars reminded them of thousands of drops of milk! In reality, this is our own galaxy* viewed from the side. When we look at it up in the sky, we cannot see its spiral shape because we are "inside" one of its arms, near the outside edge!

Our galaxy as seen "from above"

Our galaxy "in profile", as viewed from afar through a telescope*

Stars

Night lights

Stars are immense balls of electrified gas. At their core, hydrogen* transforms into another gas, helium*, which produces huge amounts of energy in the form of heat and light. The light radiates towards the outer edges of the star, making its surface bubble, and then escape into space... along with an array of little particles*. You could say that stars are like gigantic bombs that are constantly exploding, and have been for billions of years!

Pictures in the sky

Aries, Taurus, Gemini, Cancer, Leo, Virgo, Libra, Scorpio, Sagittarius, Capricorn, Aquarius and Pisces... do these mean anything to you? They are the signs of the zodiac, which are in fact constellations of stars! Imaginary lines that connect certain stars, "outlining" different animals. Why are there 12 signs? Imagine we were to draw a straight line from the Earth to the Sun; this line would point to a constellation. In a month's time, since the Earth would have revolved part of the way around the Sun, the same line would point to a different constellation. 12 times a year, the Sun pinpoints a different constellation and these are known as the 12 constellations of the zodiac.

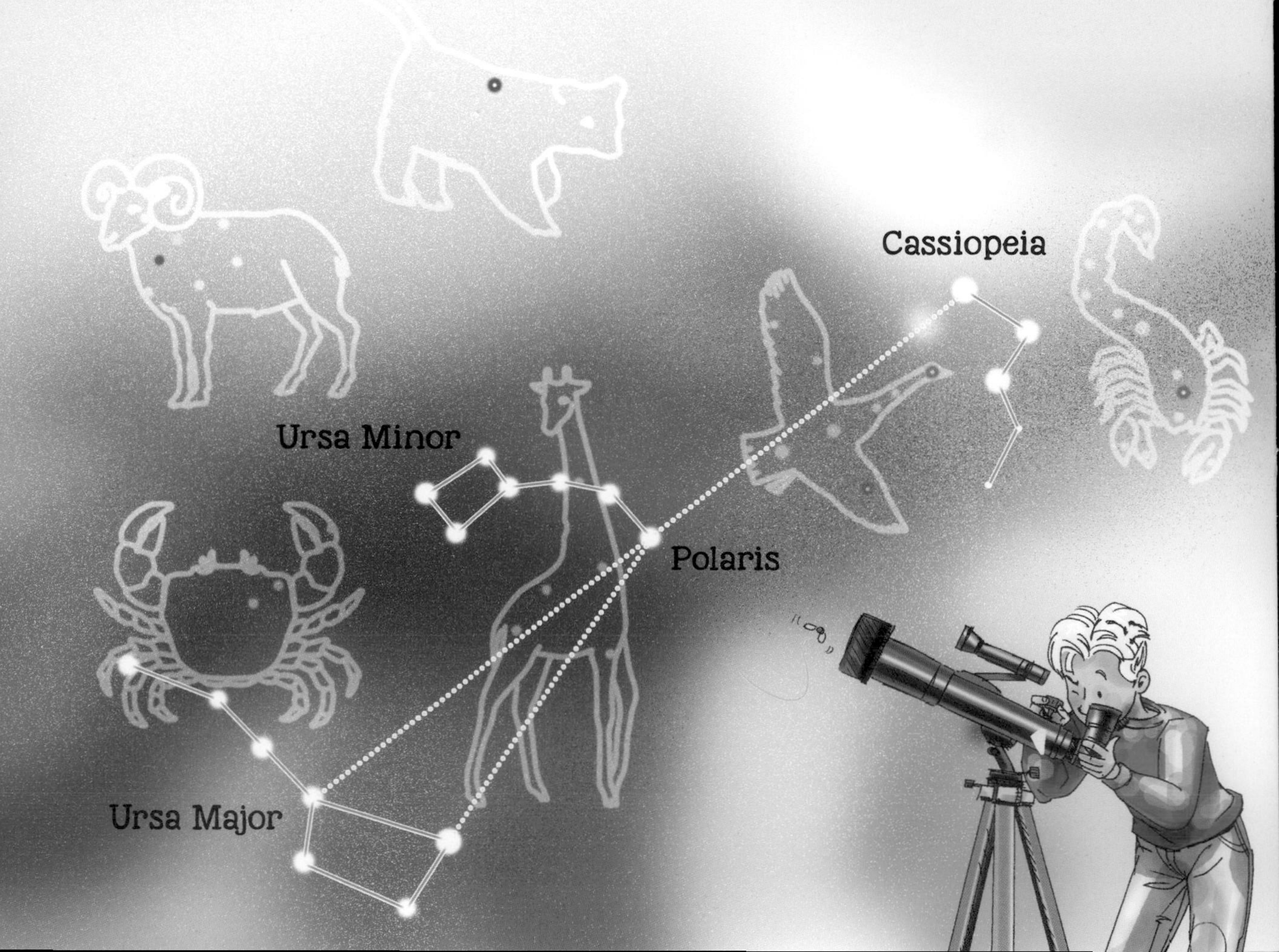

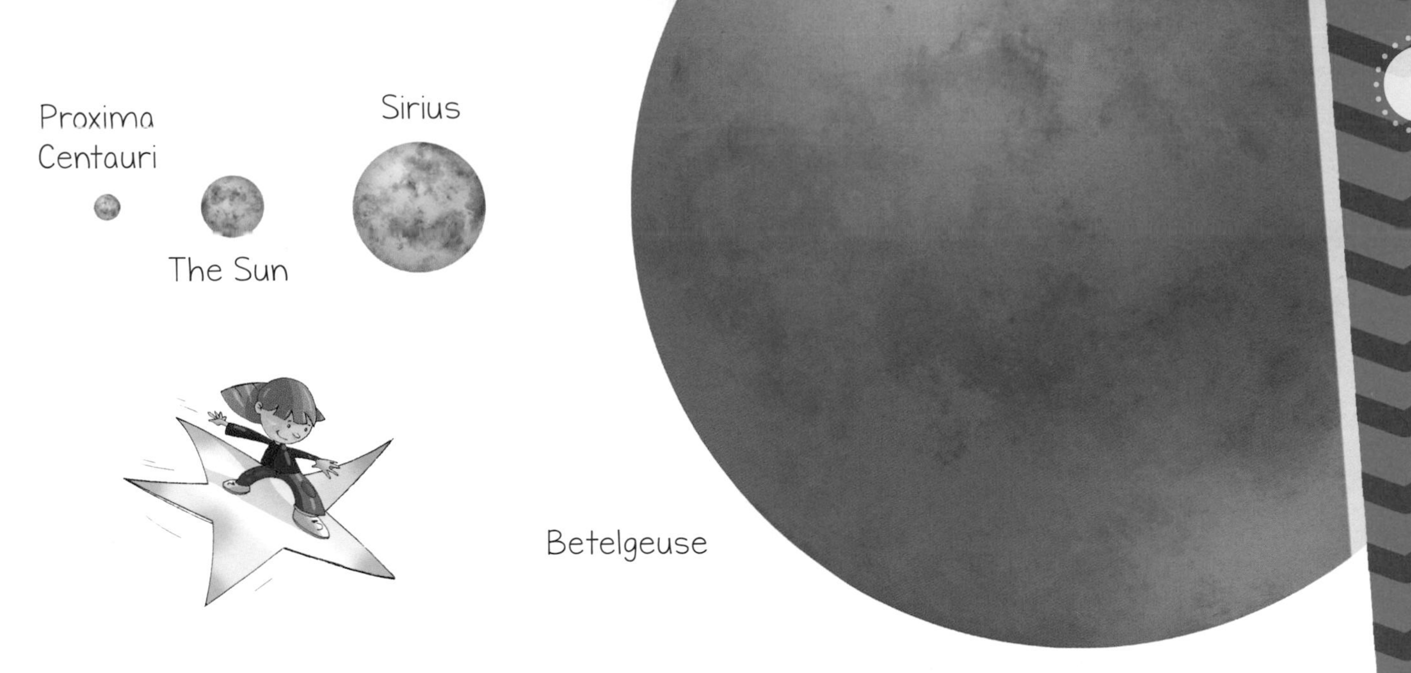

The Sun; a small star!

The difference in size between a neighboring star, Proxima Centauri, the Sun, Sirius (twice the size of the Sun) and Betelgeuse, a giant red star that shines as brightly as 60,000 Suns!

Little lights from far away

The stars are so far away that their light can take thousands of years to reach us. It is so faint when it arrives that it is drowned out by the luminous blue light of day. We therefore only see the stars at night. Owing to gusts of atmospheric wind, small clouds and circulating dust, their light appears to twinkle...

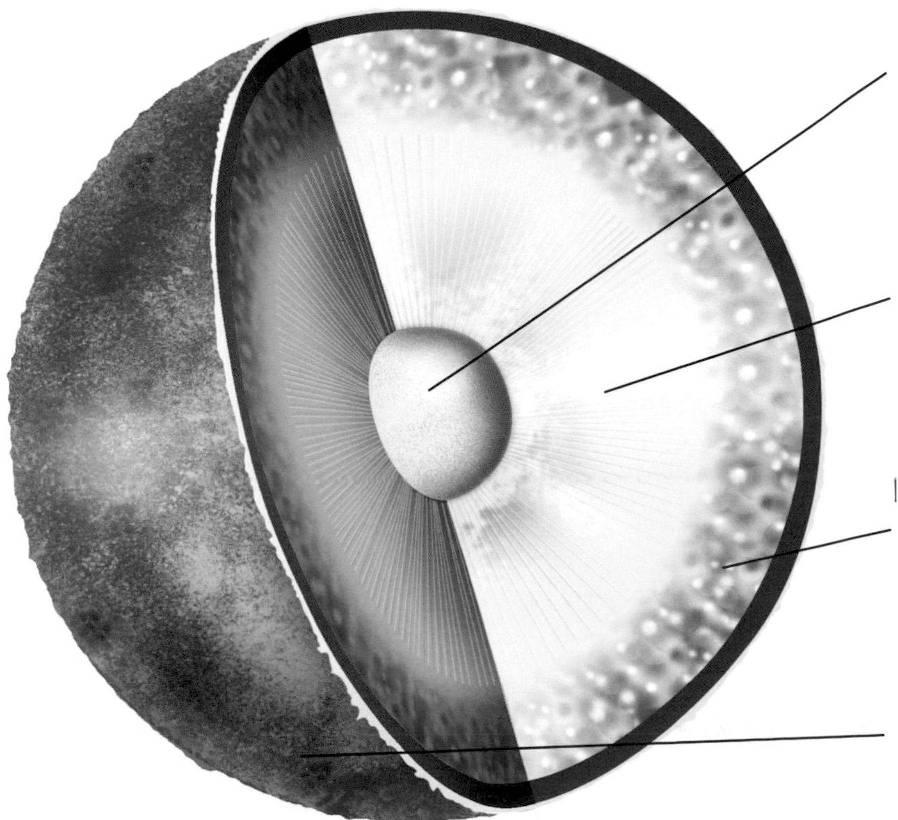

The star's core, where hydrogen* turns into helium*.

The intermediate zone that conducts the heat and light produced at the core of the star.

The bubbling zone, just below the surface.

Photosphere: the surface of the star, from which light and particles* are emitted.

The Sun

Our very own star

The Sun is an ordinary star that was born 4.6 billion years ago. It is gradually using up its hydrogen* reserves and in 5 billion years' time, when these are exhausted, it will swell up so big (becoming a gigantic star known as a red* giant). It will be so big, it will scorch the Earth! At its core, the temperature is unimaginable: some 15 million degrees Centigrade! The heat and light energy it produces escape into space, providing us with light and warmth. The Sun is 745 times heavier than all the planets in the solar system put together! These planets revolve around the Sun, attracted by this immense ball of matter.

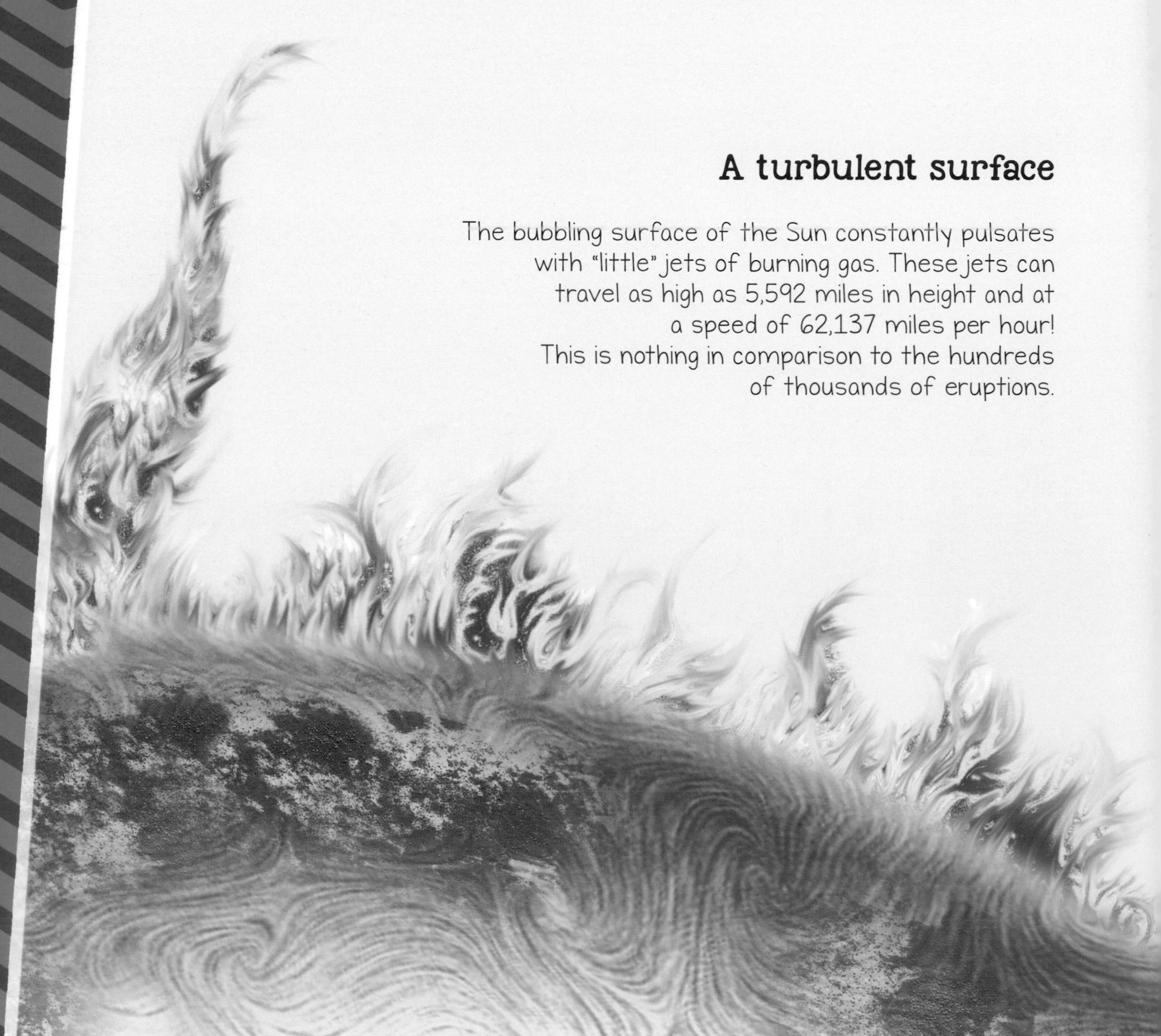

A turbulent surface

The bubbling surface of the Sun constantly pulsates with "little" jets of burning gas. These jets can travel as high as 5,592 miles in height and at a speed of 62,137 miles per hour! This is nothing in comparison to the hundreds of thousands of eruptions.

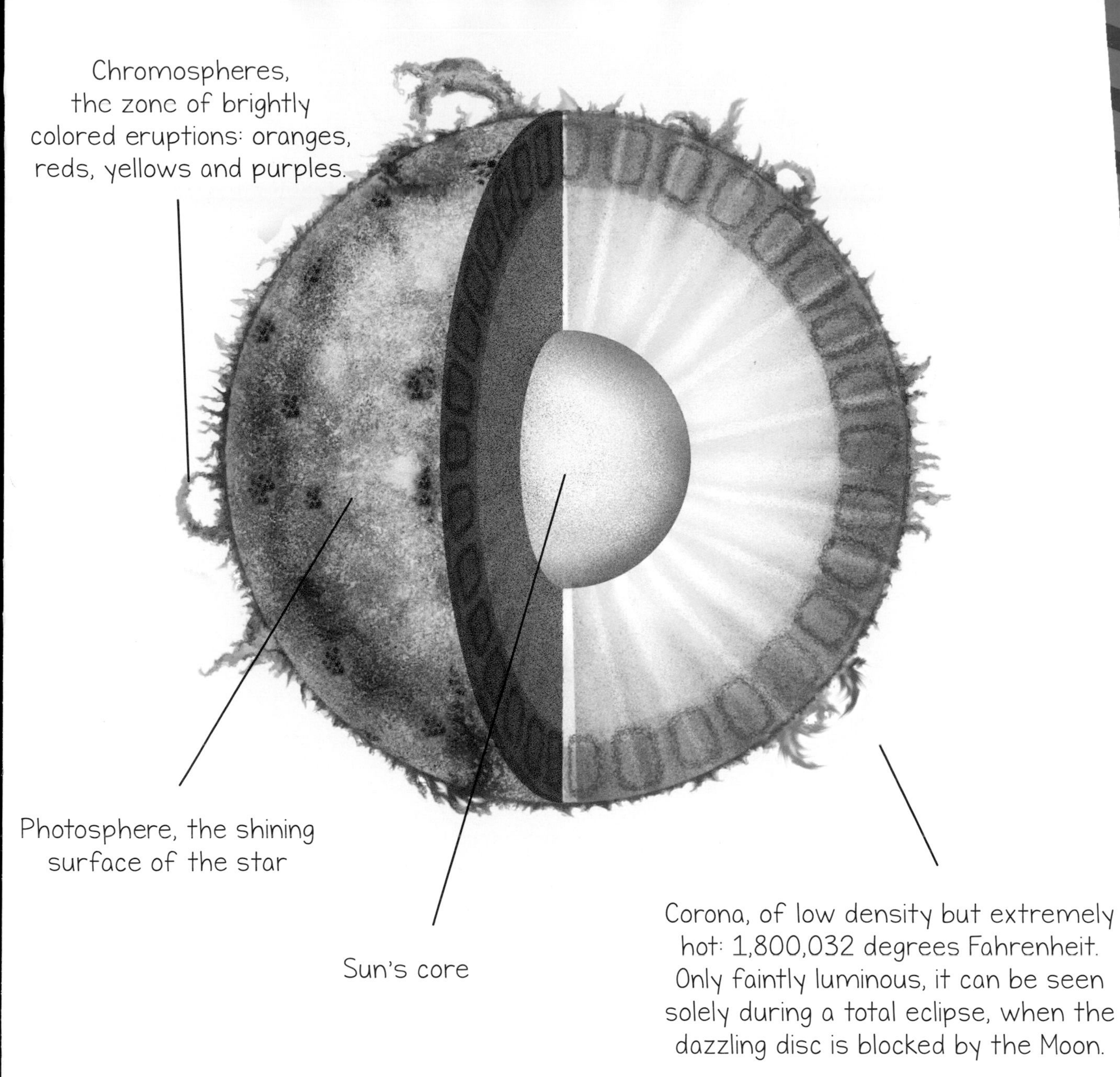

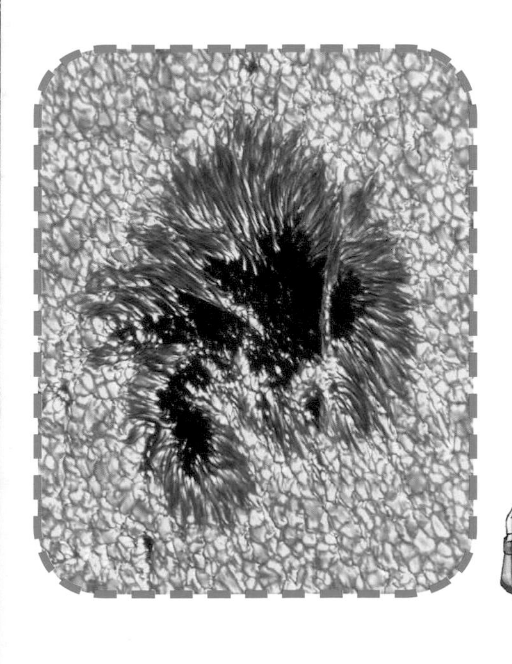

Sunspots

The surface of the Sun is hot: around 9,932 degrees Fahrenheit. In sunspots, however, the temperature is "only" 7,300 degrees Fahrenheit. For this reason, they produce less light and shine less brightly than the rest of the Sun's surface. Sunspots appear darker to us. It is thanks to these sunspots that we know that the Sun rotates. They also indicate the level of activity on a star: the more sunspots there are, the more protrusions and major eruptions there are, and the more particles* and rays the Sun is emitting.

Mercury

Mercury is the closest planet to the Sun. It races around it in just 88 days. It is a little bigger than the Moon, however, much denser and its metallic core is unusually large. Its surface is riddled with impact craters, a reminder of the million years of meteorite* bombardments to which Mercury was subjected to in its youth. Too small to have been able to retain an atmosphere, this planet endures the full impact of solar radiation. It gets really hot! The area facing the Sun can reach 752 degrees Fahrenheit, while the other side of the planet is freezing: minus −338 degrees Fahrenheit! Ice has even been identified in the craters around its north pole!

A planet full of metal

Mercury is the planet with the highest metallic content in the entire solar system. So much so, in fact, that the metal is unlikely to be natural. It is thought; that a big, iron-rich meteorite* collided with the planet, penetrating it and remaining embedded there, which would explain its large iron core. An immense crater, Caloris, is seen as evidence of this impact.

Hardly visible

Mercury lies right next to the Sun. We can only see this tiny, bright spot, which is generally drowned out by the dazzling light of our star, just after sunset, when the latter is hidden below the horizon and no longer blinds us. At this point, Mercury is visible in the dark blue of the sky, just before it too descends below the horizon. For the same reason, we can also make it out some mornings, just before sunrise.

The Solar System

Mars

Earth

The

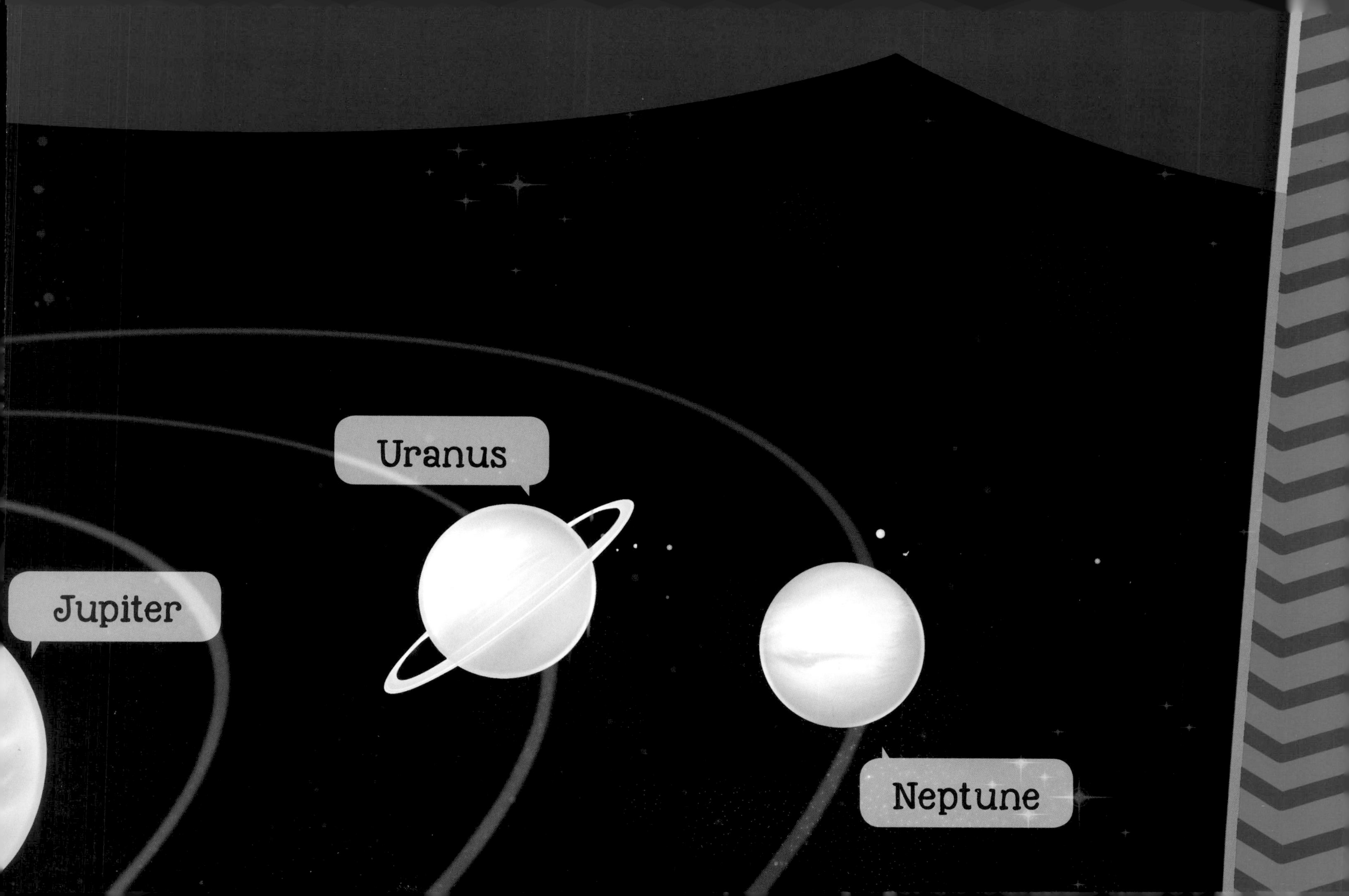

Jupiter

Uranus

Neptune

Saturn

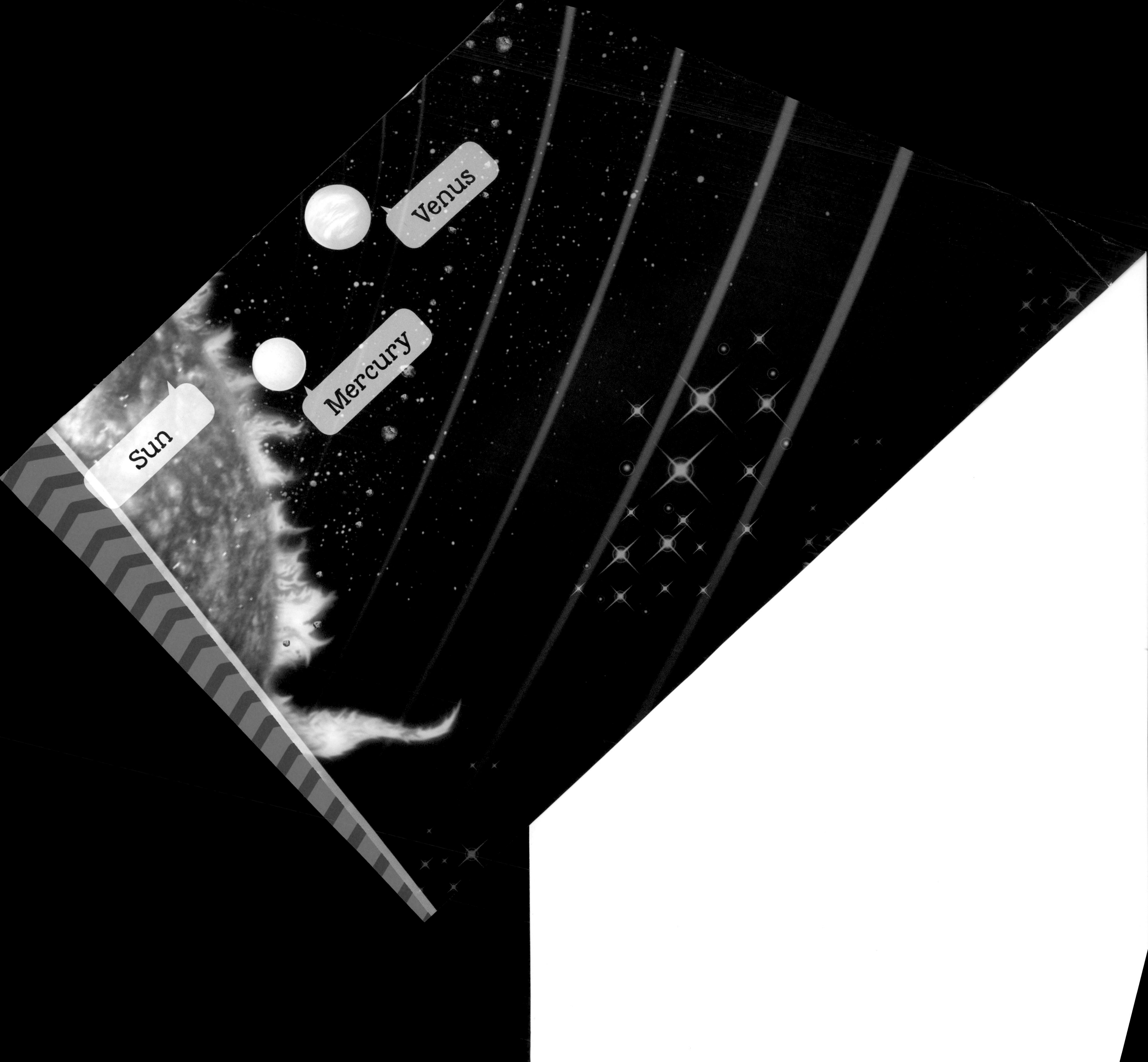
Sun
Mercury
Venus

Venus

How would you like to go for a walk in acid rain?! Venus is hidden beneath a layer of clouds 10 times thicker than Earth's, its atmosphere of carbon* dioxide is 90 times denser than ours and it is battered by violent cyclones*. Sunlight hardly breaks through! At a temperature of some 752 degrees Fahrenheit, the conditions on Venus are extremely difficult. In addition, there are thousands of volcanoes constantly spewing burning lava.

A planetary greenhouse

The atmosphere of carbon* dioxide on Venus acts in a similar way to a pane of glass: the small amount of sunlight that it lets through heats up the ground. The heated ground, in turn, emits infrared* rays that cannot penetrate the atmosphere to escape. They therefore remain trapped and the temperature of the planet continues to rise... to some 752 degrees Fahrenheit (a very hot greenhouse for sure).

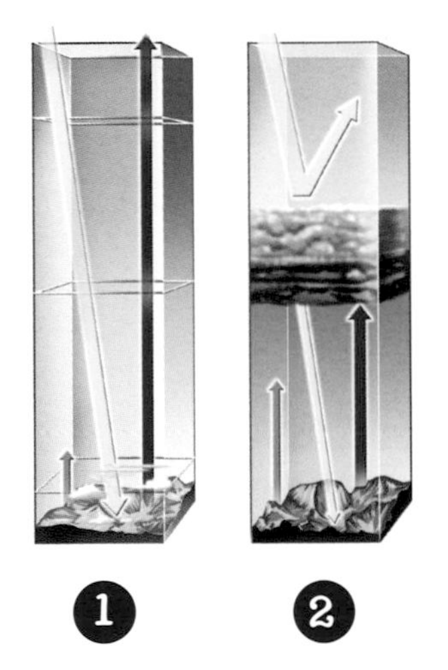

1 Earth: a great deal of sunlight (yellow arrow) reaches the ground but, since the significant infrared* produced (red arrow) can escape, very little heat is retained.

2 Venus: only a little sunlight (yellow arrow) reaches the ground, but hardly any infrared (red arrow) escapes; it remains trapped in the dense layer of clouds and continues to heat up the planet.

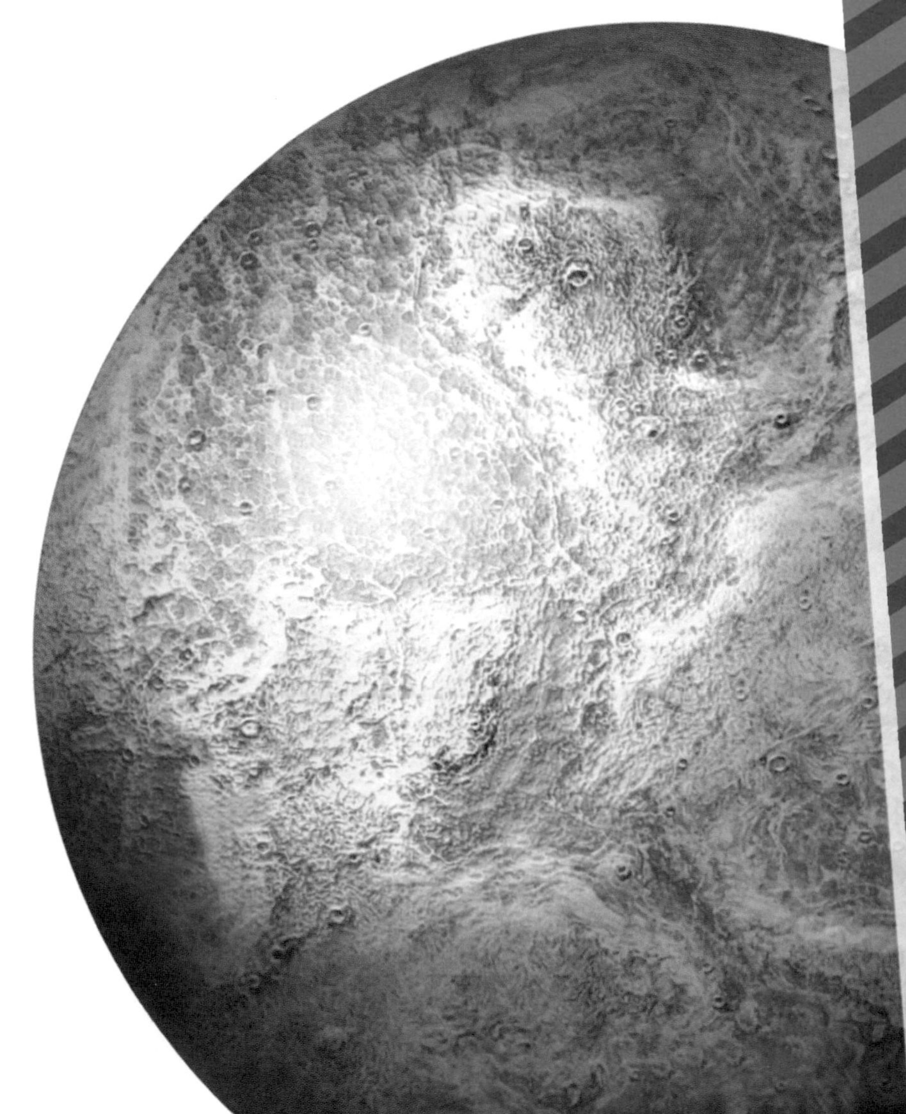

Earth

Our planet

Planet Earth revolves around the Sun at a distance of 93,205,678 miles. In addition to rock, it contains a vast amount of water, and an atmosphere (the air that we breath). This atmosphere is rich in oxygen*, which sets Earth apart from all the other planets in our solar system. Earth is truly a living planet with a great deal going on. For example, the continents on Earth shift very slowly over the course of millennia; from time to time continents become "pushed together". When this occurs, and the pressure gets too high, the pressure is released in the form of an earthquake or volcanic eruption. Storms may rage across the skies, with the rain and the wind sculpting the landscape and the rivers carrying water to the oceans. However, Earth is the only planet in our solar system to sustain life!

Air and water

If it weren't for the water that covers two-thirds of the planet, you would not be here reading this book. The sea is the source of life, and all living things contain water. The air that we breath is a mixture of nitrogen* and oxygen*, the combination that is essential for life.

The Earth is spinning fast!

In one year, Earth completes one full journey, or revolution, around the Sun. That's quite some trip! One billion kilometers a year. It makes quick progress: 18.64 miles per second (or 67,108 miles per hour). This is 100 times faster than an airplane flying at full speed. All the time, the planet is also rotating on its own axis*, taking 24 hours (one full day) to turn all the way around. As such, it completes 365 turns per year.

So why don't we fall over?

Like all planets, Earth exerts a powerful force over everything in its vicinity: balls and apples, for example, always "fall" towards its core – no matter where they are. If we were at the South Pole, we would always have our two feet firmly on the ground and anything we dropped would fall to our feet.

The Earth in cross-section

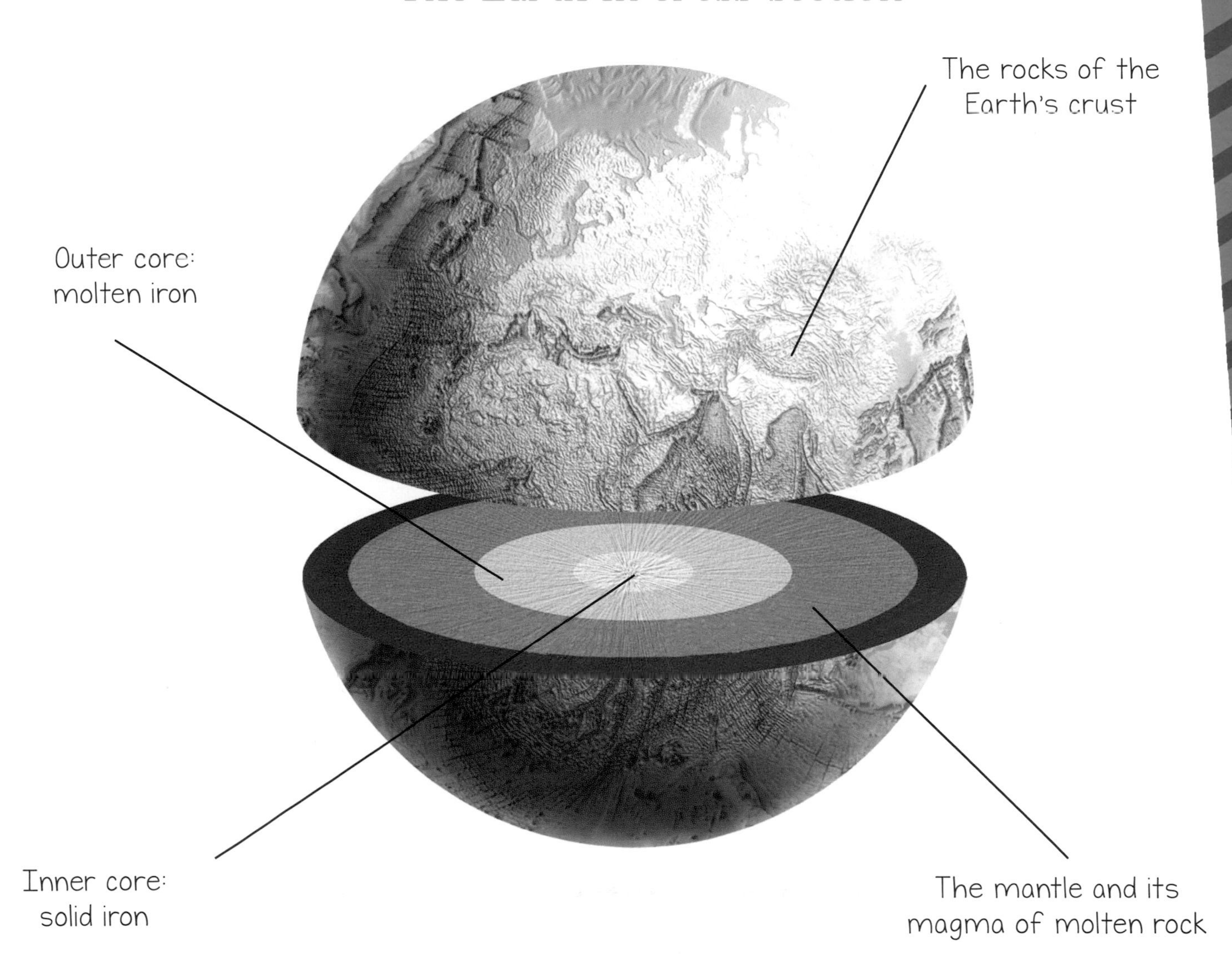

The Moon

The Moon is our only satellite. It is 4 times smaller than Earth and does not shine, but instead reflects the light of the Sun. It is "dead", riddled with impact craters from meteorites* that missed Earth! With no atmosphere to protect it, the Moon's temperature is extreme – ranging from 248 degrees Fahrenheit to minus – 428 Fahrenheit at night! It revolves around the Earth once every 28 days (in other words, one lunar day is the equivalent of 28 Earth days). The Moon always faces us with the same side, the other side remaining permanently "hidden" from our view.
Where did it come from? According to the latest research, a fireball from outer space hit Earth shortly after its formation, sending pieces of the Earth's crust flying into space. These pieces are thought to have merged to form the Moon.

Exploring the Moon

With no atmosphere, the Moon is not fit for human habitation. To walk on the Moon, astronauts must wear spacesuits that resemble deep-sea diving suits. These suites provide them with air to breath, maintain their body temperature and protect them from cosmic rays!

Viewed from the Moon, Earth is blue all over and speckled with white clouds; it floats in a black sky.

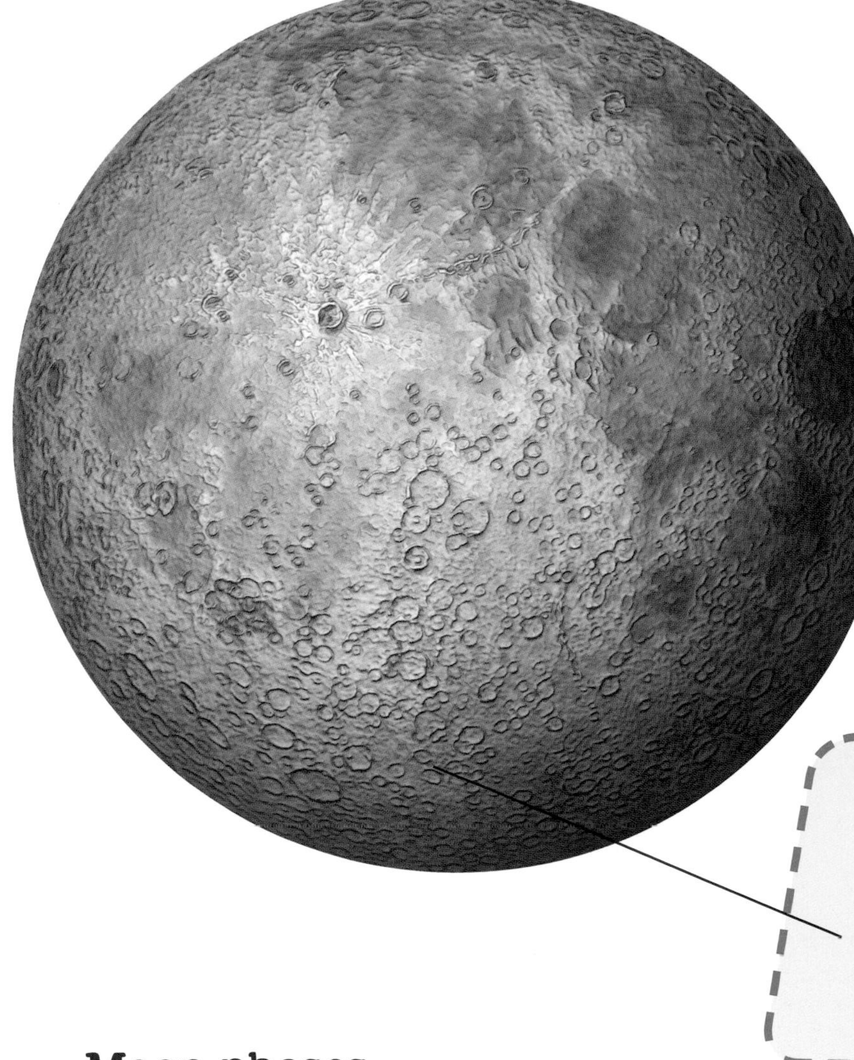

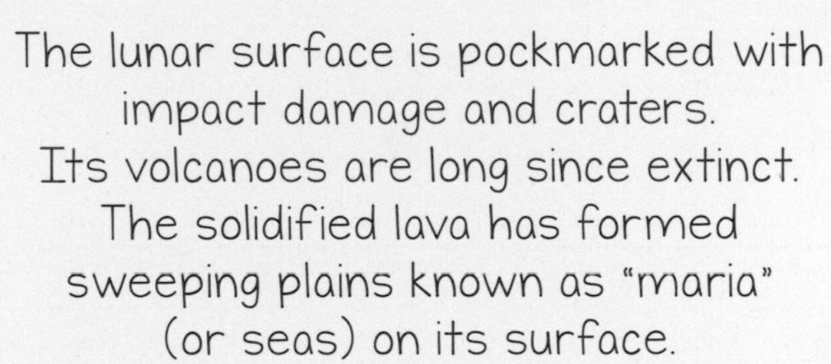

The lunar surface is pockmarked with impact damage and craters. Its volcanoes are long since extinct. The solidified lava has formed sweeping plains known as "maria" (or seas) on its surface.

Moon phases

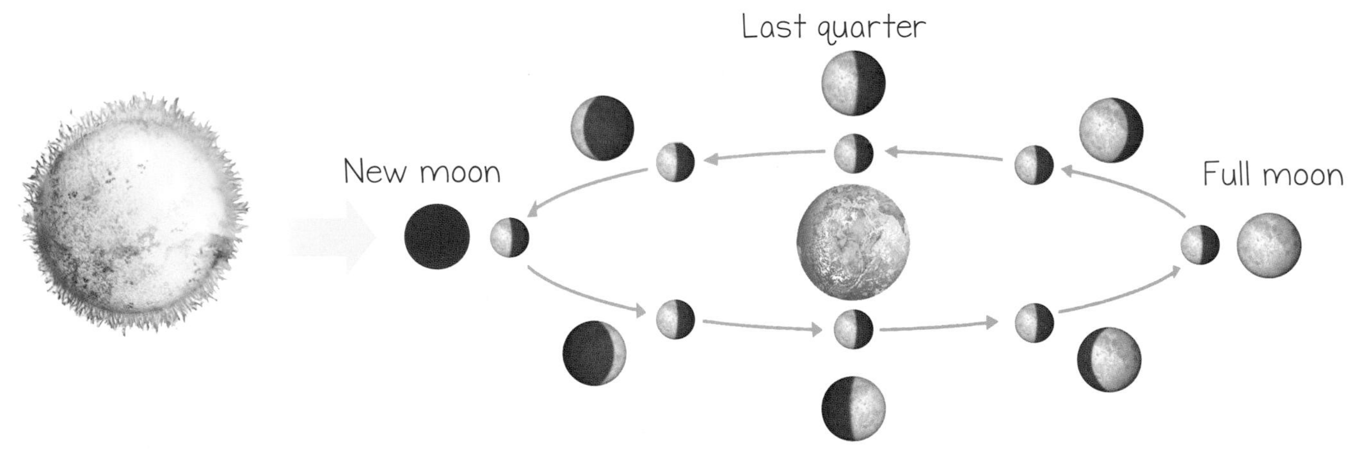

Shown above are 8 positions the Moon can be found in over the course of a lunar month (see the small moons). Permanently lit from the same side, the Moon is always half in light and half in shadow. However, the Moon's changing position in relation to Earth and the Sun means that it does not always look the same to us! Our view of the Moon at each phase is shown here on the larger moons (imagine that you are looking out from Earth at the small moons; what you would see is represented by the big moons). Sometimes we only see its lit side (known as a "full moon"); sometimes we see it side on ("first-quarter" and "last-quarter" moons); and sometimes we can't see it at all, when the side facing us is completely in darkness (a "new moon").

Mars

Our planetary neighbor, smaller than Earth, is nothing more than a great rocky desert. Its atmosphere is composed mainly of carbon* dioxide and its red color derives from its rocks, which are rich in rusted iron! Mars has the biggest volcano in the entire solar system. It is 15.53 miles high and is 3 times taller than the highest mountain on Earth! However it is long since extinct. The surface of Mars is covered with ravines made by rivers that dried up long ago, but which remain as testimony to the historical presence of water. What happened to the water? Did it evaporate into space? Is it still there, stored in ice caps or underground? This is a real mystery. However, where there is water, there may be life! Recently a small frozen lake was identified at the bottom of a crater.

The red planet carries the name of the Roman god of war, Mars, because it is the same color as the earth from which the Ancient Romans extracted iron to make their weapons.

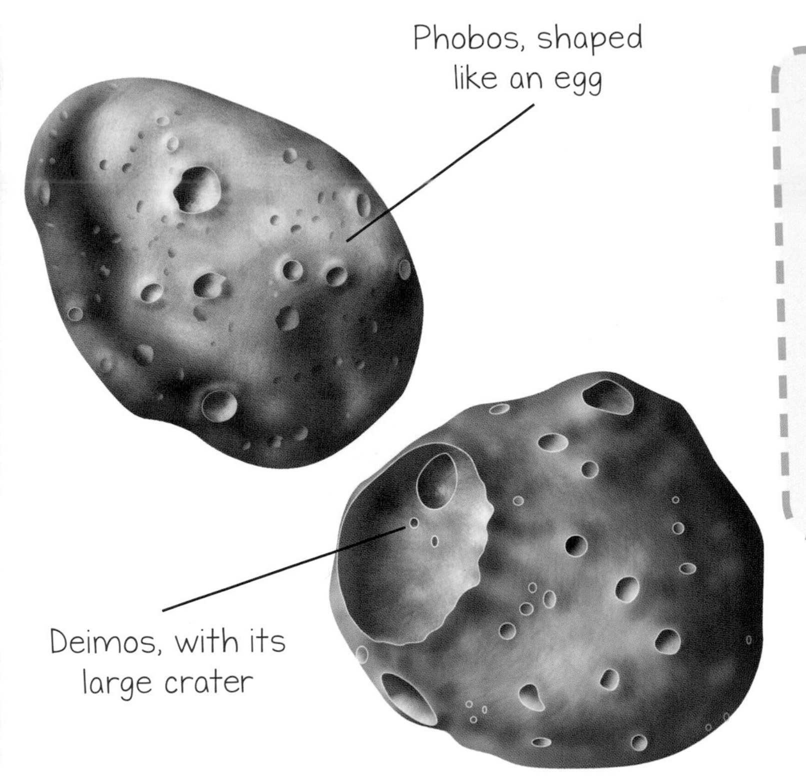

Two satellites

The 2 satellites of Mars are named Deimos and Phobos after servants of the god Mars. They are small astronomical bodies, pitted with impact craters, and measure no more than about 6.21 miles in diameter*.

For a long time we believed that Mars was home to a Martian civilisation. We no longer hope to find more than a handful of microbes there. But even that would be amazing: to find life on another planet!

Precious planet

Mars probes* have already sent back beautiful pictures of rocky desert surfaces, and in 10 or so years' time, Mars is set to be the first planet to be visited by man. Yet as the one-way trip will take more than 6 months, the key hurdle to overcome is more psychological than technical. The astronauts will have to live in close quarters, without ever being able to go out for a breath of fresh air. A few squabbles can be expected!

Jupiter

Jupiter is the largest planet in our solar system: you could fit 1,300 Earths into it! It is visible to the naked eye – almost as bright as Venus. This planet is entirely formed of gas, mainly hydrogen*. The atmospheric* pressure is so high that first it takes on the form of liquid, and then it is found as a solid form, the deeper into the planet it is found. However, there is much fluidity between the 3 phases.
At 36,032 degrees Fahrenheit, Jupiter's core is extremely hot. Its atmosphere is full of ammonia* clouds and is shaken by violent gusts of up to 373 miles per hour. Nothing on Earth could resist such a force! In 1979, the Voyager probe* discovered that Jupiter has very fine rings. We also know that Jupiter permanently emits radio* waves, as if grumbling.

The Great Red Spot

The Great Red Spot is a huge cyclone* with winds up to 248 miles per hour. It is twice the size of Earth. This cyclone has been raging for more than 300 years.

Jupiter's satellites

There are approximately 60 satellites, of which the following are the largest:

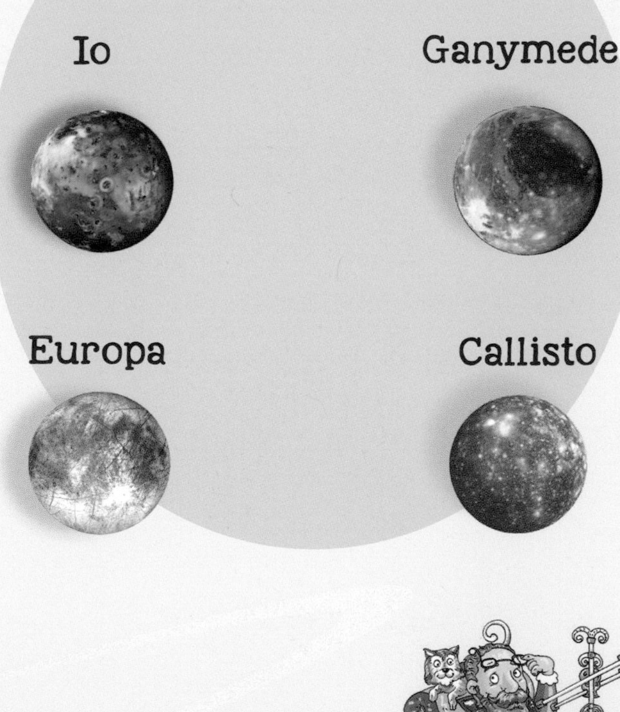

Galileo, the great Italian scholar, couldn't believe his eyes when in 1610 he looked through the telescope* that he himself had made, and saw small stars that appeared to be accompanying Jupiter on its journey! Galileo had just discovered the planet's 4 biggest satellites!

Saturn

Composed of 3/4 of hydrogen* and 1/4 helium*, Saturn is the least dense of the planets. Imagine an ocean big enough, that this planet would actually float on it! This magnificent celestial body is known most notably for its rings: a very narrow disc, just a few hundred feet thick, surrounds this planet. It measures some 186,411 miles across (a bit like a ring of tracing paper just a tenth of a millimeter thick around an object with 984 feet in diameter*!) The rings contain chunks of ice ranging in size from a few centimeters to a few meters. Their origins are unclear: could they be the result of large satellites shattering following collisions with comets* and meteorites*? Titan is Saturn's largest satellite. It has a temperature of about minus −356 degrees Fahrenheit and has a very nitrogen*-rich atmosphere... like Earth.

Saturn's satellites

Saturn has some 60 satellites. The biggest, Titan, was discovered in 1655, with the next 4 (Tethys, Dione, Rhea and Iapetus) identified towards the end of the 17th century.

Saturn's rings

There are 7 main rings: A, B, C, D, E, F and G. They contain so little matter that if they were all pushed together, they would measure less than 62 miles in diameter*.

Uranus

This ball of rock and ice does not have a very clear internal structure. Its gaseous atmosphere is mainly composed of hydrogen*, with a little helium* and a touch of methane*.
It is the methane that gives Uranus its distinctive dark blue-green color. Uranus sets itself apart from the other planets on account of its very tilted axis*.
No doubt the result of a major collision during the course of its history.
The Voyager 2 space probe* revealed 10 of its 27 satellites, along with 9 rings of dust and ice.

Voyager 2

The Voyager probes* launched in 1977 went on an incredible journey, taking in Jupiter, Saturn, Uranus and then finally, in 1989, Neptune - passing dozens of satellites and rings on the way! In order to achieve this voyage of discovery, NASA engineers took advantage of a particular alignment of these 4 planets that only occurs once every 176 years!

Neptune

Neptune's atmosphere is primarily made up of hydrogen* and helium*, but also water, ammonia* and methane*.
This planet – named after the Roman god of the sea – has 13 satellites, 4 very dark rings and winds of up to 1243 miles per hour at its equator. There is also a great dark spot and a small dark spot. Within its methane-rich atmosphere, astronomers have spotted a small white cloud that orbits* the planet every few days; they have dubbed this the "scooter"!

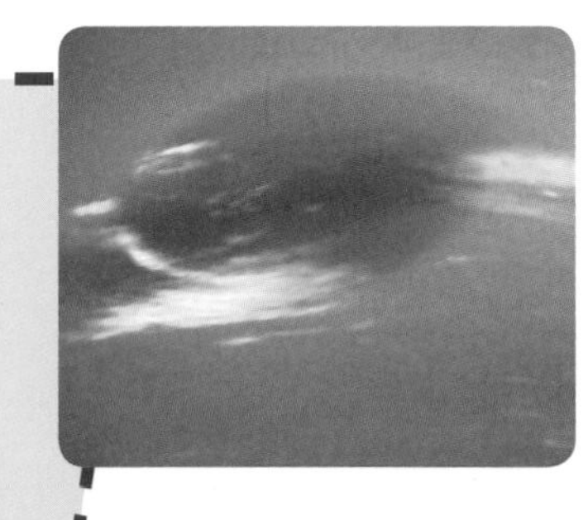

The Great Dark Spot

This is a massive cyclone*. Its white clouds form small, feather-like waves that do not persist from one of Neptune's revolutions* to the next.

Pluto: no longer a planet

In 2006, the International Astronomical Union decided that Pluto, which was truly one of a kind (much smaller than the other planets, with a very different kind of orbit*), could no longer be considered a planet, but instead belonged to a new category of bodies: dwarf planets.

GLOSSARY

Ammonia
A gas found on Earth as well as on other planets. Its molecule comprises nitrogen* and hydrogen*. When dissolved in water, it forms an alkaline solution (which can be used as a cleaning product).

Asteroid
A small rocky body travelling around in space with a multitude of others, roughly between the orbits* of Mars and Jupiter – a zone known as the "asteroid belt".

Atmospheric pressure
Air is light but it does weigh something. Atmospheric pressure is the weight of the column of air immediately above a given spot. At sea level, atmospheric pressure is around 1kg par cm^2; this drops with increased altitude.

Axis of rotation
A spinning top rotates around its shaft (its axis of rotation). An object can spin without having a physical axis, such as an ice skater doing pirouettes on an imaginary axis that runs down the middle of his or her body. Similarly, the Earth rotates on an imaginary axis that links the northernmost and southernmost points on its surface (poles) by way of its core.

Carbon dioxide
A molecule of carbon dioxide contains carbon and oxygen*. It is released into the atmosphere when we burn wood, coal or gasoline and is partially responsible for the greenhouse effect.

Comet
A small, roving astronomical body. Instead of following more-or-less circular orbits* around the Sun, the path of a comet resembles a stretched oval. When near the Sun, comets shed water vapour and dust, leaving a sparkling trail of cosmic* dust in their wake (hence the name, which stems from the Greek "komêtês", meaning long-haired).

Cosmic dust
Small pieces of debris whirling around in space. Comets* release quite a bit of this as they approach the Sun.

Cyclone
A huge storm with high winds and clouds that turn in a spiral (hence the name, which stems from the Greek "kuklos", meaning circle).

Diameter
The imaginary straight line passing through the middle of a circular or spherical object, from one side to the other.

Galaxy
A vast consolidation of stars, planets, solar systems, cosmic* dust and gas... A galaxy comprises billions of astronomical bodies that are held together by the law of universal gravitation and that, together, form a unit.

Helium
A very simple, very light gas that can be found in abundance around the Universe, notably in the stars – including the Sun. Its name, in fact, derives from the Greek "hêlios", meaning sun.

Hydrogen
The simplest, lightest and most abundant gas in the Universe, particularly in the stars.

Infrared
The Sun emits visible colors as well as others that are not apparent to the human eye, such as infrared rays. Consider the colors of the rainbow (red, orange, yellow, green, blue, indigo and purple). Infrared can be found at one end of the spectrum, before red (and just after radio* waves). Invisible ultraviolet can be found at the other end, after purple.

Meteorite
A cosmic rock, small or large, that impacts with a planet. On entering Earth's atmosphere, a meteorite will ignite and becomes a shooting* star. When they hit the ground (especially on bodies with no atmosphere, such as the Moon), the largest meteorites create craters.

Methane
A very simple gas, abundant in the Universe, the molecule of which is formed of carbon and hydrogen*.

Nebula
An astronomical body without clean contours. This term can be used to denote a variety of things ranging from a single gas cloud or a small, dying star in the process of evaporating (a so-called "planetary" nebula) through to an irregular group of stars (a faraway galaxy*).

Nitrogen
A gas that makes up 4/5 of the air we breathe.

Orbit
The trajectory that a planet takes around the Sun, the Moon takes around the Earth, an artificial satellite takes around an astronomical body, or one star takes around another... Orbits are most often elliptical, but sometimes almost round.

Oxygen
A gas component of the Earth's atmosphere that is essential for life (respiration). A molecule of water, which is also essential for life, is made up of one atom of oxygen combined with two of hydrogen*.

Particle
A general term for a minute portion of matter. Atoms* are examples of particles, as are their smaller constituent parts: electrons, protons and neutrons.... The Sun is constantly sending tons of particles out into space; this is known as the solar wind.

Probe
An artificial satellite sent on a fact-finding mission within our solar system. Probes can be sent to orbit* other planets or to land on them.

Radio wave
The Sun emits light waves (which we can see) and other waves that are invisible to the human eye, such as radio waves. Our radios pick up artificial radio waves and turn them into sounds that we can hear. It is possible, with a special radio, to pick up radio waves coming from the Sun, Jupiter or elsewhere in space; these sound a bit like a cross between gale-force winds and the noise of a deep-fat fryer!

Red giant
The stage at the end of a star's life when it balloons exponentially, giving out a red light. Our sun will become a red giant in 5 billion years' time.

Revolution
A complete lap of one astronomical body by another.

Shooting star
Not actually a star, but a cosmic rock (or small meteorite*) that is drawn towards Earth and bursts into flames as a result of air friction.

Supernova
A Latin word describing a very brief stage in the life of a large star in which the star explodes and/or its core implodes! This is one of the most violent and bright phenomena to take place in the Universe.

Telescope
Regular telescopes provide us with close-up images of faraway stars and planets, drawing on the visible light they emit. Radio telescopes also give us close-up images, but these images come in the form of radio* waves that are emitted by certain astronomical bodies and invisible to the human eye.

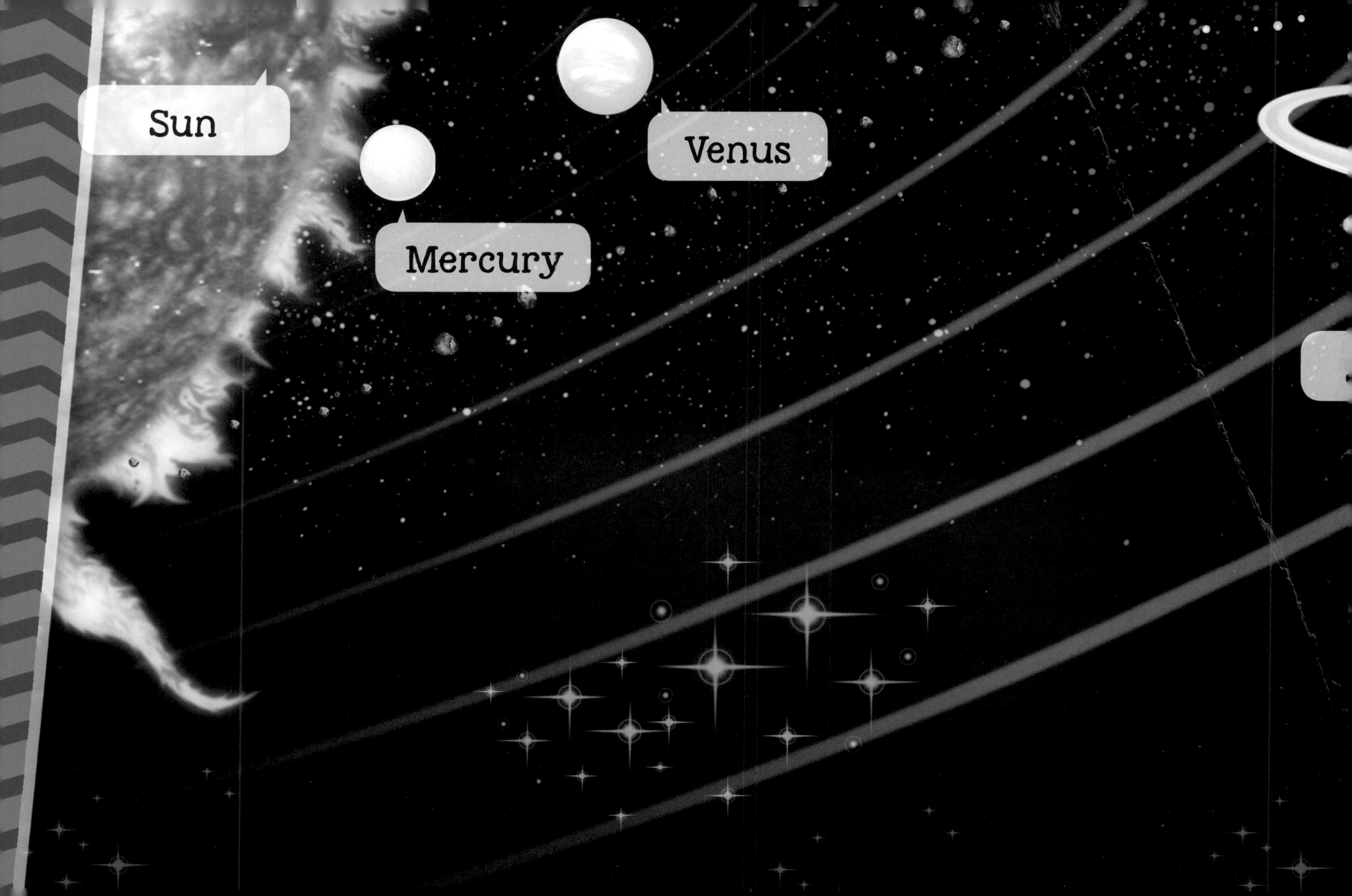
Sun
Mercury
Venus

Saturn